HOTEL HORRORS & *HALOS...*

and other unforgettable hospitality moments

BOOK ONE

A MEMOIR BY

Jeannine Connor Gittens

Edited by Lil Barcaski

Published by: GWN Publishing

www.GWNPublishing.com

Cover Design: Kristina Conatser Captured by KC Design

ISBN: 979-8-9863922-5-7

This book is dedicated to my two sons. You're the most precious and rewarding joys of my life. I thank God for allowing me the honor of being your mom!

CONTENTS

INTRODUCTION

I'm Jeannine... just a gal from St. Croix, US Virgin Islands. I've always been intrigued with the fine art of travel and meeting new people from all around the world. My years enduring a tumultuous and highly dysfunctional childhood were spent hoping that one day I would escape the insanity. Addicted to reading, I was often scolded by my elementary school librarian, who threatened not to allow me to check-out more than 10 books at a time. (Yes, I said 10.) But there was something surreal in those pages. I loved reading about faraway places and learning about different cultures, customs, and languages. As a pre-teen, the desire to see these places and meet diverse people tugged at my heart-strings and never let go.

At my elementary school, a blended, academically talented class (ATC) was created for outstanding students. I spent 4th through 6th grade in that ATC environment and then skipped the 8th grade as well. I got A's without even studying. Instead, I would lock myself in my room and read books, magazines, encyclopedias – anything I could get my hands on—all while listening to the likes of Michael Jackson, Madonna, New Edition, Wham, and Phil Collins (you get the picture—I was an 80's kid.).

My having so much brain power, meant that everyone had an opinion about what my future career track should be. Behind their backs, I sneered at the many adults who told my mother that a successful career in education, law, medicine or some such field was surely inevitable. I would just roll my eyes, scoff at the thought, and continue trying to find a college where I could study Travel and Tourism.

In a pre-Google age, that proved to be quite tedious. No one in my family understood my zeal and they were not thrilled about my intended major. I eventually graduated from high school with many honors, but no college fund. I persevered and, by divine intervention, I discovered a small private college in Ft. Lauderdale, Florida in late 1990. I was quickly accepted to the dual major program of Business Administration / Travel and Tourism Management.

With only a small scholarship in hand, and ginormous faith, I boarded a jet for the first time ever in January of 1991. I left St. Croix only one week after turning 17 and headed off to college in South Florida. This was the first official step towards pursuing my destiny.

Since that day, I've enjoyed a colorful and intriguing journey in the hospitality industry. In this book, I share my personal experiences, spanning almost two decades and many area codes, working in airlines, hotels, and luxurious private villas.

If you're thinking of a career in hospitality, I hope to inspire and accurately inform you about what it's like behind the scenes. If you're simply passionate about travel and are usually a guest somewhere, this book gives some insight into what management and staff must endure just to make you happy. No matter your interest, this alphabetically designed memoir is full of laughs and sobering food for thought. I hope you enjoy reading this as much I enjoyed writing it!

—A—

ALIGNMENT

Put Pressure on Your Passions

As I alluded to in my introduction, my desire to study Travel and Tourism was not met with resounding joy. To put it frankly, the adults in my life thought I was nuts. I first fell in love with this industry while volunteering at my uncle's office, Connor's Car Rental, on the island of Anguilla during my summer vacation months.

Also a pilot, my uncle had many friends from all around the globe. As a girl, it was exciting to meet people with unique accents and diverse fashion trends; their perceived happiness mesmerized me. I always asked them where they were from and, if I didn't understand their language, I would boldly ask what they were speaking. I fantasized about visiting the Netherlands, Canada, New York, Switzerland, Morocco and all the other amazing places these tourists hailed from. At age 12, I mentally set out to make that happen. By age 17, I was already well on my way.

When I finished studying in Florida, my first degree in hand, I was determined to get a job with an airline and see the world. I quickly found out that this was easier said than done. For months, I stayed in Florida and applied to countless airlines by mail, only to receive disappointing replies. I even started applying to cruise lines, but the responses were all the same. My degree meant nothing to these companies because I didn't have a little thing called EXPERIENCE. Eventually, I returned to U.S. Virgin Islands and started calling local airlines and travel agencies. Frustratingly, I was met with the same response. By then, I had started pursuing my Spanish degree at the University of the Virgin Islands on St. Thomas and had built up quite a resolve. I was determined not to take 'no' for an answer.

One day, while on a weekend break at home on St. Croix, I called a fairly new airline and asked if they had any vacancies. The first question was, of course, if I had any experience. I had nothing to lose, so I told the gentleman on the phone that I actually had zero experience, but I had a passion for the industry and a degree to prove it. I promised him that even if he let me just volunteer, I would be an asset to his company. There was dead silence on the other line. After a few seconds, he said that he was totally impressed by my spunky attitude and, while he couldn't make any promises, he wanted to meet me the following week. I prayed that the job was already mine. I just had to go get it!

I went back to St. Thomas with a spring in my step and only one goal: to get hired by that airline! I didn't even care about my university classes. The following week, I walked 30 minutes from the university campus to the airport. I was a bundle of nerves by the time I shook the man's hand at 10 a.m. (I later found out he was the Vice

President of the company!). He told me that in an un-precedented decision (and surely in a pre-9/11 world), he had decided to let me volunteer at the airline for one week and that he'd take it from there. I wanted to shout and do a cartwheel, but I remained composed and simply smiled with gratitude.

He introduced me to the operations manager, a vibrant, chain-smoking Antiguan lady, who seemed eager to train me. Within about three hours, I was answering calls and looking up flights in the system for actual customers on my own. It felt so natural. My Intro to Linguistics and Spanish Literature classes were the furthest thing from my mind. I was in absolute heaven! The day sped by and before I knew it, 5 p.m. arrived. It was a bittersweet moment. I'd just had one of the best days of my life and, for me, it ended way too soon. I thanked the VP, bid my trainer a good afternoon, and walked back to the university campus.

The next day I returned to the airline's ticket counter, 20 minutes early, after another 30-minute walk. I waited patiently to be let into the Reservations office. Just then, I saw the VP coming out of the office door; he looked at me with a strange expression on his face. I felt my heart thumping against my chest as I said good morning. He just stood there; cobalt eyes sternly fixed on my face.

Hesitantly, he said that there was a bit of a dilemma and he needed to talk to me about it. My mind raced nervously as I tried to remember if there was anything I might have done wrong the day before. I guess he saw the scared look on my face. At that point, he chuckled and then told me what could only be described as sweet music to my ears. He explained that after I'd left the day before, the trainer told him that I was one of the fastest learners she'd ever encountered and, in her opinion, I should be hired immediately and forget all that "volunteer bullshit." He offered me a job on the spot and this time I could not contain myself. I jumped for joy and even hugged that bear of a man. In that moment, my world felt divinely aligned; I thanked God for answering my prayer.

That job blossomed into a whole new world of opportunities for me. I worked with the airline for many years and even moved to their Daytona Beach, Florida headquarters. I eventually lived with the airline owners in a fly-in community and became the Reservations Director. It all happened because I put pressure on my passion.

We are each born with a purpose, but sometimes it's difficult to figure out just what that is. One key to discovering your purpose is to examine the things you are most passionate about. In life, not just in this industry, if you want something badly enough, the word no should only be an acronym for "next opportunity." When you put pressure on your passions, you will experience a sense of fulfillment and alignment. It'll just feel right.

(And yes, I eventually got my Spanish degree... but from Florida International University. ¡Olé!)

—B—

"BYE, FELICIA!"

(Actually, "Bye, Mr. C.!")

My feel-good story of how I landed my first airline job came with some behind-the-scenes pain. The Vice President of the company, who hired me, soon returned to the States after feeling confident that he'd selected a great team in the Virgin Islands. I was sad to see him go because he was a great motivator and I was forever grateful to him for giving me a chance. One of the other reasons I hated to see him leave was that I was left at the mercy of the station manager, a lanky and lecherous man I will refer to as Mr. C.

I had no prior knowledge of this guy except for the fact that before I became an employee, he would always hit on me whenever he saw me hanging around the airport. Naturally, I always ignored him. An older man with allegedly wanton ways when it came to young women, he was of absolutely zero interest to me. I just knew him as the manager guy from the airport who had a really strange, gliding walk.

He had been in training on the mainland when I was hired, so when he returned to work and saw that I was the newest employee, he seemed beyond thrilled, probably thinking he would be able to seduce me (dream on, mister!). He started out being kind and patient with me, making me feel right at home. Soon he began offering me a ride back to the university, which I always refused. He bought me lunch a few times which I grudgingly accepted. Then he started scheduling me to work the early morning shifts to be alone with him. As annoying as he was, I always handled myself professionally.

Eventually, he got tired of the game that only he was playing. So, he flipped the script. Instead of being gracious to me, he started picking on me and blaming me for incidents that were not my fault. He would have staff meetings and not include me. He would go out of his way to avoid me. At one point, he wickedly omitted my name from the schedule for a whole week. I was so distressed, and because I was the youngest and newest employee, I felt I couldn't complain this creep to anyone. All I could do was pray about it.

One rainy morning, about a month into working at the airline, I arrived at the airport for my shift and saw the entire staff standing around the ticket counter. I timidly walked up to the group, said good morning and asked if everything was okay. They somberly told me that Mr. C., our "beloved" station manager would no longer be with the company and that the next day was his last. I don't think I did a very good job of hiding the bliss that erupted from me. Although the sky was cloudy that day, all I could feel was sunshine glowing inside of me. I was ecstatic! That was the best darn news I'd heard in weeks!! I went straight into the back office to work as the other employees stood around outside lamenting. I giggled and thanked God for answering yet another prayer. Mr. C. left the next day and I wanted to throw a party. I never saw him again.

Some call it karma. I call it divine intervention. Things always have a way of working in your favor. Sometimes the best course of action is to take no action. If you're honest and true, many times you will reap direct rewards of your good heart and hard work. Staying focused is key. No one has the right to force you out of your blessing. In this instance, because of Mr. C.'s nasty ways, I had seriously considered leaving a job I loved. I'm so glad I didn't.

—C—

CULTURAL CALLALOO

As a Caribbean islander, I dare to say we see the world differently. In an age where racial tensions are insanely high and discrimination of every kind seems prevalent, I am proud to say that in the Caribbean, we tend to embrace and glorify uniqueness. To me, my Caribbean culture is like callaloo—a word used in the Virgin Islands to describe the sumptuously mixed gumbo-like dish made of fish, crab, other meats like smoked turkey or pig tail, okra, spinach, other vegetables, and various spices. (In other places, from Jamaica to Guyana, callaloo is referred to as the leafy, spinach-like vegetable that is eaten alone or mixed into other dishes.)

Working in hospitality provided myriad opportunities to have "cultural callaloo" experiences up close and personal any given day of the week. It's hard to get bored when you consistently meet amazing people. I've met people from every continent except Antarctica. (Although I did have a guest who'd flown there once.)

There were two specific cultural "blendings" that have stayed with me over the years. The first was the wedding of a Nigerian man and his Malaysian fiancée who flew in from New York. The group did a property buyout at the boutique villa property I managed, and what a grand affair it was. Before they arrived to the island, the father of the groom placed an order with me for approximately $30,000 worth of wine and spirits. That was just the tip of the iceberg. The most intriguing part of the wedding event was the effortless blending of these two very distinct cultures. At one point, I felt like I was watching "Coming to America" meets "Crouching Tiger, Hidden Dragon" in living color.

The highlight of their five-day stay was the tea ceremony, which was held before the actual wedding day. I was left speechless after witnessing this serene ritual. It began with the bride and groom-to be, sitting side by side in two regally decorated chairs while all of their guests and family members presented them with gifts. Both sides of the family donned their respective cultural attire and each person or couple patiently lined up to offer their verbal blessing and gift to the couple. The colorful, flowing parade of exquisite adornments included hues of shimmering golds, dazzling reds, crisp whites and invigorating greens.

And as for the gifts? I'm not talking Tupperware and Amazon gift cards here. I'm talking diamonds, sapphires, envelopes with wads of cash, raw gold, etc. There was so much wealth in that room, I'm sure the total value of their gifts could buy an island or two! When the tea ceremony ended and the party headed off to dinner, they left someone behind to guard the two safes which held the glorious valuables.

My second, and absolute favorite experience, was with a family from Florida. When they arrived to the property, I stood there grinning like an idiot, totally speechless. The first person to step out of the taxi was an almost seven-foot, 40-something ebony man with flowing dreadlocks. (Not too many times in my private villa career had I seen that!) Behind him was his family—a petite, olive-skinned woman with stunning Chinese features, a sophisticated Indian woman, who appeared to be a sexagenarian, and three gorgeous cinnamon children ranging from pre-teen to about 16. Then another couple stepped out of the taxi—a buxom, perfectly coiffed Eartha Kitt look-alike and a bouncy Chinese man who appeared to be in his late 50's, with an old-time dial radio perched on his shoulder.

I knew from my pre-arrival consultation, that this was a family. It was only after I welcomed them, and they started to speak did I realize that they were from the Caribbean. A stunning family hailing from both Trinidad and Jamaica. The dreadlocked man and his wife were the parents of the three children. The wife's mom, whose Indian ancestors had been in Trinidad for generations, had married a Chinese-Trinidadian, producing their beautiful daughter. The other married couple comprised another Trinidadian beauty, aunt of the main guest, and her Chinese-Jamaican husband. (If you've not had the pleasure of seeing a Chinese man chanting dancehall music, skanking to ska, and belting out Bob Marley lyrics, you are definitely missing out!). I spent an awesome week with this family and just learning some of the history behind their family tree was priceless.

I am grateful for the years I have spent working in an industry that expanded my mind in such unforgettable ways. I feel as though a lot of the hate and ignorance in our society today stems from lack of exposure. We are all unique, and if we could learn to appreciate that fact, I think the world would be a much more pleasant place in which to coexist. I think a good place to start is asking questions, respectfully, about things that you're not extremely knowledgeable about. If there is no one to ask, do your own research and educate yourself. Ignorance is not bliss. Racism and discrimination are as bad as any malignant cancer. Learning to be open, tolerant, and accepting of others has many rewards. Without a doubt, a successful career in hospitality is one of those rewards!

—D—

DOUBLE D'S

Meeting Mr. & Mrs. DeNiro and other high-profile guests

Working in the superluxury sector is tedious. If you're not detail-oriented, thick-skinned, and physically able to work ridiculously insane hours, stay away. However, in spite of all of the drama and stress, there are days that make every ankle blister worth it. One perk (some may say, detriment) of the high-end hospitality life is meeting celebrities. It's always a test of your professionalism when you see one of your favorite stars, but still have to remain cool, calm, and collected. This happened to me with Mr. and Mrs. Robert DeNiro.

A local travel professional, known for handling very high-profile clients, called me up one day and said a chef was scoping out exclusive properties for his boss. Our property was next on his list to visit. I met the chef and gave him a villa tour. He kept muttering to himself, as he counted bedrooms and seemed to make a mental checklist of where the primary guests and other accompanying staff would stay. I was excited, but didn't want to get my hopes up because I knew he was visiting quite a few villas.

Within 24 hours, I received another call from the local agent, stating we'd been chosen. Of course, this person still refused to tell me who the actual guests were. As the General Manager of the property, I found this rather insulting and also very scary. I decided that it really didn't matter who the guests would be because our service standard was for each and every guest, not just A-listers.

The staff of the mystery guests checked in a few days later. They shopped for specific ingredients, prepped meals, security-checked the villas using their own lists, rented vehicles and cell phones, etc. On the day of the "big arrival", I went down to the villa and did a quick run through to make sure things on our end were in place – villa office was stocked, internet connections were solid, all suites, public areas and pools were spotless, bath amenities were stocked to par, welcome rum punch made, etc.

While keenly checking the kitchen, I noticed two cell phones on the breakfast bar with two post-its with "Mrs. D" and "Mr. D" written on each one. Though wildly curious, I knew better than to ask any questions. I would meet my guests soon enough. And sure enough, within 10 minutes of my final walk-through, a large black Escalade pulled up to the villa. I held my breath, desperate to see who would step out of the tinted taxi. When a very tall, elegant black woman stepped out of the car, I felt lightheaded. I vaguely remembered seeing her face on TV not long ago.

As I waited to see what other secrets the stately vehicle held, I saw one Mr. Robert DeNiro stepping out from the front passenger seat. I didn't know if I could contain myself. I bit my lip to stop myself from screaming. It's not like I had never met celebrities in the past, but I really love "Bobby D" in all his cinematic fire and so does my husband. This was going to be an EPIC week, I thought. And it truly was. They were the nicest, calmest, most thoughtful and unpretentious "celebs" I'd ever met. But during their stay, I had one of the most hilarious and unforgettable incidents with Mr. D.

I was so thrilled that one of my all-time favorite actors was staying at the property, I actually went to work at 5 a.m. just to be in my office in case they needed anything. I was told Mr. D. was an early riser. One morning, I took it upon myself to walk over to the villa and start cleaning up the exterior pool deck from a late-night dinner they'd had the previous evening. From experience, guests leave behind glasses, plates, wine bottles, wet towels, and all sorts of other items (think sex toys) on the deck. I didn't want a single out-of-place item on that deck when Mr. and Mrs. D. woke up. Yes, the villas staff is paid to do all that, but I was already there. For me, when it comes to getting the job done immaculately, titles and positions are irrelevant.

Just as the sun made its debut, I noiselessly scurried into the villa laundry room with some damp towels in my hand. It wasn't even 6 a.m. yet and I was as quiet as a mouse. The coast was clear and I felt a sense of accomplishment. As I emerged from the laundry room, on tip toe, I heard a strange noise in the main villa kitchen. Being just a few feet away from the laundry room entranceway, I decided to peek into the kitchen to see if something was wrong with the fridge or the dishwasher.

As I turned the corner, I collided with Mr. DeNiro—dressed in his white robe, apparently making coffee. I blushed and stuttered a profound apology as he laughed heartily at my apparent discomfort. I apologized for the seeming intrusion and explained that I was just doing an early clean-up until the appropriate staff arrived. He waved away my words and told me not to worry. He even offered me a cup of coffee, but I graciously declined and literally ran back to my office after exiting the villa.

The rest of the week was a dream. Mrs. DeNiro was a true southern belle and spoke with me about emerging health care at the time, such as thermography, as I drove her to tennis. I admired the way Mr. D. took time out to go to the beach every morning and spend quality time with his son. In all of my years working in the industry, meeting this kind and endearing couple, was one of the biggest highlights. It is one experience I will never forget. I'm sorry they're currently divorced, but life goes on.

There are other experiences that were also mesmerizing in their own way. One fun experience was having Mariah Carey's bodyguard tell me that working in Anguilla was always so boring for him because he never got to roughhouse anyone or pull anxious fans off of Ms. Carey. He told us that Japan was probably the craziest in terms of fans and he enjoyed going there because he actually got a chance to work! And by work, he meant "beat people up." Yes, really, he said that.

Anguilla, known for attracting celebrities, is a haven for the rich and famous because there is a level of respect and reverence that is very hard to find elsewhere. In Anguilla, people do not run after recognizable faces for autographs and selfies. That is highly unusual. If you're rushing into your fave Mexican restaurant for take-out dinner and happen to bump into Queen Latifah (as I did), you simply smile, apologize and bid her a good evening. If you see Michael Jordon riding a bicycle near your office one morning, you wave and go back to work. Having lunch or dinner on the beach and run into Denzel, Ellen DeGeneres or Steve Harvey? Be cool. I remember a friend who said she almost fainted when meeting Sir Paul McCartney.

Villa staff is also trained in the art of keeping their lips zipped and are not allowed to discuss anything about in-house guests with other in-house guests. How did we handle having Glenn Beck and Katie Couric staying in side-by-side villas during the same week? Say nothing and simply let them have the pleasant surprise of finding out they are "vacay neighbors" while sipping cocktails and chilling with their families on the same beach.

—E—

EMPLOYEES FROM HELL

Yes... I went there. One of the drawbacks to working (anywhere) are those individuals you get to spend most of your time with for 40 or more hours a week. Your workmates can really make or break your day. I have worked with some of the most amazing, ride-or-die, dependable-to-a-fault, people who have become lifelong friends. And then I've worked with people who would make me wonder if they were raised in a zoo or if they'd escaped from a mental hospital. This chapter is dedicated to the latter. (Naturally, the names are changed to protect the not-so innocent.)

LAURA: I remember reviewing this young woman's resume and thinking she was too perfect to be real. The included photo on that resume showed a stunning face that could grace any fashion runway. Her educational achievements were off the charts for someone just shy of 20. I have to admit that her youthfulness did raise a bit of a red flag, but after working with so many stubborn, stuck-in-their-ways, mature employees, I was ready to train someone with a virginal mindset. Or so I thought.

She had worked quite briefly at an inn and was terminated without warning while still in the probationary period. During the interview, I asked her what had happened. She told me that the female supervisor didn't like her because of her striking looks and the fact that guests gravitated to her, tipping her regularly and very well.

Knowing the way things went down in the islands, I didn't find this hard to believe. I did my part, however, and called the owner of the property to find out her take on my potential new hire. She simply told me that there was a lot of shenanigans surrounding the situation but she thought I should hire the gal.

I pondered it for a few days and called the innkeeper, who'd been off-island. He told me bluntly that Laura was crazy and very unstable, and he thought she needed to get her head checked. Never one to hold my tongue, I paraphrased the innkeeper's remarks and asked Laura during interview #2 what she thought of those comments. She told me that the innkeeper had tried to hit on her and became enraged because she refused his advances. Again, knowing that this was a sad norm in the islands, I stupidly believed her and hired her the following day. And that began a ridiculous saga that would have driven any sane person to the bottle!

Laura started off with a charming personality. Her quick and witty ways were impressive. Excellent on sending grammatically correct emails (you would not believe how HARD it is to find someone to do that!) and a winner with the guests. I was thrilled. So thrilled, that about a month after she started working, I decided to take a week off and visit my family.

Two days later, I got a phone call from a deranged sounding female who eventually identified herself as Laura. She said she'd had a blowout fight with her parents and was delirious with the stress of it all and wanted to quit her job. I told her to calm down and call me back when she could speak rationally.

When she did—the very next day—she told me that she had moved out of her home and was staying with her friend. I still couldn't figure out why this was my problem or my business (as long as she showed up for work on time and didn't actually quit), but because of my nurturing side and, being a mother myself, I felt sorry for this young lady.

And so did our company CEO. She'd moved to a new location on the extreme other end of the island and had no car. The CEO, who lived in that area, told the young woman that he could take her to work daily and one of the other employees could take her home in the evening until she figured something out. The only catch was that this man went to work at 6 a.m. daily without fail and even though her shift started at 9 a.m., she'd have to leave home at sunrise if she wanted his help. Surprisingly, she agreed and came to work daily at 6 a.m., snoozed for a few hours on the staff room couch and then got dressed for work in the office bathroom. (I know it feels like I'm going really slow with this, but I'm at the point where you need to sit up and pay attention.)

For the first few days of this carpool arrangement, I would go into the office bathroom—which by the way was a lavish full bathroom with marble floors, double sink, Kohler rain-head shower, large vanity and dressing area—with a bit of annoyance. Over the years, the senior management team took turns ensuring this bathroom was always spotless and stocked with hygiene essentials. There were so many times we'd had suffer through 15-hour days and this was our solution to freshen up between shifts. This restroom was our baby, and we took care of it with pride. The property housekeepers seldom ventured into it because it was always pristine. However, this was all about to change for the worse.

One day, I walked into our majestic bathroom after Miss Laura had used it for her morning ritual and literally fumed. Shoes were scattered on the floor, bath towel in the sink, her hairbrush and toothbrush on the vanity, makeup everywhere, her shampoo and bar of soap sitting on the shower floor. I blinked twice in speechless horror, reversed out of the door and made a beeline for her desk. I asked her if she could please tidy up the bathroom, which also doubled as a visitor bathroom if we happened to have property tours, travel agent inspections, etc. She graciously apologized and went to clean up the bathroom.

Her actions were repeated the next day and the day after that. I finally told her to either get her act together or I would forbid her from using the bathroom in the mornings. I said this in front of our CEO, who seemed equally confused and appalled, just so that he was made aware of this ongoing situation. She batted her mile-long lashes and, in a coquettish manner, apologized once again.

Two days later, I went into the bathroom just to make sure it was clean, as we were having a VIP site inspection and that's when I almost fainted. There was a used maxi pad sitting atop the waste basket, face up, with specks of blood on the tiles in front of, and on the lid of, the toilet seat.

I wailed like a banshee and told Laura to get her ass in the bathroom and clean it up—with Clorox—immediately! In the seven years I'd worked at this particular property, I had NEVER experienced anything like that and with the other office staff on vacation, it was just this nasty child and me. It was like a slap in the face. I gave her a lecture not only as her boss, but as a mother. She sat silently and listened to my rant without uttering a word, but from that day, she spitefully turned on her "bitch switch." The Laura I had interviewed on day one was replaced by the true psychopath she was.

There were so many crazy things this young woman did after that day, it is a jumbled blur in my head, but here are some of the ones I actually had to document:

- She blocked my email address and marked it as spam, so that none of my emails with vital directives would go to her inbox. Because I had full control over all accounts, I eventually found this out after I did a forensic check of her email.

- She tried to convince the President and his wife that she was an innocent, talented, prodigy and I was the mean, evil witch of a boss who was jealous of her and couldn't stand her (remember what I told you she said when I asked her why she was fired from the first job at the inn? If not, go back and read the start of the chapter.)

- She started smoking weed and would come to work stoned at 10 a.m. with her long wavy hair stinking of ganja smoke. One shake of that mane and the whole staff could be high in seconds!

- Apparently raised as an only child, and in a manner akin to a princess, the girl had no idea of what neatness was. The wastebasket under her desk was always overflowing and even the housekeepers would complain about how nasty she was for such a beautiful girl. Doritos bags, cookie and chewing gum wrappers, breadcrumbs, and Coke cans were always floating around her space—and she sat at the main reception desk most days. Written warnings were moot. Because of her, we had to call in the exterminators for the entire office.

- She started hanging out regularly with a coworker who was definitely NOT her friend. At one point, there was a viral recording, done by the other employee, Radience, of Laura talking about her sexual adventures and mishaps (I don't know which was worse: hearing Laura speak of swallowing cum or the fact that Radience secretly recorded their conversation in the first place, and shared it).

Eventually, Laura and her family reconciled, and they moved to another country. I can honestly say I was relieved and wished her well. Once she was gone, I called back the innkeeper of her first place of employment and told him I was so sorry I didn't listen to him in the first place.

MORAL OF THIS CHAPTER

Listen to the former employers of people you may want to hire. They usually hit the nail on the head and can save you oodles of stress.

—F—

FAM TRIP DISASTERS

Familiarization trips are organized for travel industry professionals to experience a property or activity in order to sell it to their clients. These trips are usually free to the attendees with an array of activities and presentations planned. Most times, this is a highly successful endeavor, and the results can be tracked and evaluated.

Sometimes, however, some real losers slip through the cracks and aren't even worth the name printed on their business cards. Such was the case with a particular fam trip organized to bring together six esteemed luxury villa agents. There were stringent guidelines these agents had to follow. One guideline was the fact that no one was allowed to bring along a personal guest.

Prior to the agents' arrival, our property received a profile on each of them and their respective company. One Hamptons-based agent, who I'll call Tawny, was particularly enthusiastic about her upcoming visit and called our office a number of times to ask specific questions like where the largest suite was located, which suite provided the most privacy, were any of the villa pools heated, how late would staff be on property, etc. We thought she was being diligent and asking questions for a client. Boy, were we wrong!

When the group checked in, instead of six agents (all of whom were to be women), there were seven people and that odd additional person was a man! The rep from the Tourist Board office seemed equally uneasy, but offered no explanation other than the gentleman was from Tawny's office.

I was left to the task of welcoming the agents and giving the usual orientation and villa tour. Almost immediately, Tawny brashly blurted out that she was going to have a mini-vacation and long overdue honeymoon with her HUSBAND (yes, that's who this guy was!). She claimed that the oversized master suite was theirs and no one had a say in it. She then promptly took her speechless husband by the hand and disappeared into the room with a pitcher of our complimentary rum punch in tow. The other agents were so stupefied, they just stood there with their mouths agape.

That entire weekend proved to be quite dramatic. This woman made everyone else on the property feel like her servants and skipped all the presentations and group activities we, as the hosts, had planned. Tawny may have been categorized as a super-agent, but for me, the only thing she seemed super at was being crass and ghetto-fabulous. Most of her time was spent at the pool with her two-sizes-too-small bathing suit while her hubby slathered her translucent skin with sunscreen, trying hard not to get it into her brashly-dyed blonde tresses. Needless to say, we never got any bookings from her and

I later learned that her travel agency was permanently closed.

Another fam trip memory was a little bit more embarrassing on the side of the property. A group of journalists was staying for a few nights to write about exclusive private villas as well as the island nightlife scene. Their pub crawl bus was scheduled to pick them up at 10 p.m. since every Caribbean nighttime lime seems to start after 10:30 p.m.

(By the way, in the Caribbean the word lime isn't merely a fruit. It's how we describe the fine art of partying. You can use lime as a noun or verb. Example: "You missed a great lime last night at the Beach Club!" Or "I'm still tired from liming all weekend.")

Anyway, back to this disaster.

The fam trip group was dressed and ready to lime. The bus arrived and, for some reason, our property gates were all closed. This never happens as one gate is always left opened and guarded when guests are in-house. The driver began to toot the horn to alert the security guard to open the gate. No one came out, and the gates remained closed.

By this time, the fam trip group was standing outside of the villa, wondering why their bus was idling outside of the property gates, honking the horn, and not pulling up to the villa to let them hop on. Eventually, the group leader walked up to the bus and realized that they were literally locked inside of the property. Each guest room was equipped with a list of emergency numbers. Calls to the security guard went unanswered, so guess who was next on the list?

Just as I was hopping into my pajamas, my cell phone went off and this bizarre story was relayed to me. Within seconds, I'd roused my husband out of his sleep, tugged a sweatshirt over my head with flip flops on my feet and begged him to drive me to the property. When I got there, about eight minutes later, I found the gates open, a sheepish-looking security guard, and a group of amused journalists. I am pretty sure they saw the steam coming from my ears.

Apparently, our guard had decided to slip into an unoccupied room at another villa to take a nap, not knowing the guests were scheduled to go out. By locking the gates, he thought he was protecting them and covering his tracks. He admitted all of this in a jumbled waterfall of barely intelligible words. It was the worst night to drop the ball; he was fired the next day. Lucky for us, we received glowing reviews and the locked gate incident never made it to print.

—G—

GAY MAYDAY

In the early 2000's, before the Caribbean tourism sector warmed up to the idea of mainstream LGBTQ+ travel (and when it was just the letters LGB), I worked at a forward-thinking, luxury property where the idea of absolute discretion was drummed into our psyche on a daily basis. We also shared the ideology that everyone is deserving and worthy. And to whittle it down even more, my training embraced the idea that your bedroom business is just that... your business. But as the days counted down to our first LGBTQ group arrival, and me not being able to say a darn thing about it to anyone—not even the staff—daily panic attacks became the norm for me.

Unlike most of my colleagues, I had lived and worked internationally and made friends with many people from all different walks of life. However, I knew how homophobic many Caribbean people were at the time. I proactively pondered how to handle any questions that could possibly come my way after the group checked in.

The group of 10 arrived, with nine men and one woman, for the five-bedroom villa for five nights. Most of the staff assumed it was a family holiday because the guys were so comfortable sharing rooms. I worked efficiently as always and kept my mouth shut. The first few days went by without a hitch and the jubilant group quickly became friendly with all of the staff. They hit the beach, hung out at the pool, enjoyed the butler service and round-the-clock premium cocktails, went on island excursions, and were, overall, fabulous guests. Regardless of whether the staff had figured it out or not, I was very proud of the fact that they offered the group total respect and outstanding service.

With only one day left, everything was running smoothly. That is, until my head gardener stepped into my office one afternoon gasping for breath, clutching his chest, and sweating profusely. All he kept saying was, "Help me, Jesus! Help me, Lord Jesus."

At first, I thought he was having a heart attack. I asked him if I should call an ambulance, but he vehemently shook his head. I ran to get him a glass of room temperature water and a damp washcloth to cool him down. I'd never seen such a dark-skinned man turn pale before. I didn't think it was biologically possible. It was the strangest metamorphosis ever! He sunk to his knees and started wailing like he was injured.

I calmly spoke to him and asked him to tell me what had happened. He kept rubbing his eyes and slapping his cheeks, but could not speak. I was perplexed and worried. Could it have been a big snake he'd seen in the garden? Had he broken one of the custom Italian wall sconces around the villa? I just couldn't understand what could have evoked such an outburst from this typically relaxed man.

After about 10 minutes of trying to cajole him into telling me what the heck happened, he finally started to speak. Never in a million years could I have imagined what he said to me. The words that came out of his mouth made me want to run for the seashore or fall on the floor in a fit of raucous laughter.

This is what went down: he was tending to the villa's rooftop garden at about 11 a.m., located adjacent to the top floor master suite. He said that as he watered the flower bed, he began to hear a squealing sound over and over again. Assuming that most of the guests were either finishing breakfast downstairs, on the beach or relaxing by the pool, his initial thought was that an animal had gotten into the villa somehow and was unsuccessfully trying to get out. He recounted how he quickly jumped over the privacy ledge, which afforded a partial view into the master suite. Lo and behold, there was no animal in the room, but rather two gentlemen having sex... missionary style. The "squealing" was apparently from one of the men, in the throes of passionate lovemaking.

I sat in my chair speechless, eyes closed, and tried to wrap my head around what this reserved uber-religious islander had just told me. I wasn't too happy that this imagery was now etched into my brain. What people did in their bedrooms—straight, gay or anything in between—was not my business. I really hated the fact that the gardener made it my business that day. I opened my eyes and looked at him then. He was in obvious mental distress, so I told him he could leave for the rest of the day and to take the next day off as well. He graciously accepted my offer and literally ran from my office, making a beeline for the staff parking lot.

I sat there stupefied for about 20 minutes. I worried that the guests may have seen the gardener on the roof, assuming he was spying on them. I thought about him telling his story to just a few people, having it spread quickly across the entire island (which is usually the norm) and all the possible backlash from this very reserved, mostly-Christian community.

Grey Goose and I became acquainted for the first time that day. And I mean really acquainted! I'd never had vodka before that incident. The guests left the next morning and they all assured me they'd had the best time ever. (Whew!) They were beaming and I was truly happy that they'd enjoyed our property and the island. I later found out one of the gentlemen was the president of a Fortune 100 company. Everything had gone smashingly, and all was fine. But as for my gardener, he was never quite the same after that day. He asked never to be assigned to the rooftop gardens again.

—H—

HOLIDAY
HEARTACHES

One of the most frustrating and unavoidable things for anyone working in hospitality, is the fact that the industry never sleeps. This is something that really got to me over the years. When I was single, I'd work 60-80 hours a week at my airline jobs without thinking twice.

After I got married and had kids, every holiday became an opportunity to make memories. And I'm a sucker for making memories—I still am! But it usually meant I was away from my family during the most precious days of the year. In typical hospitality fashion, I was always busiest during Easter, Christmas, Boxing Day, New Year's Eve, Spring Break, Thanksgiving... all the times of year where family bonding means so much.

Intense sacrifices came with the job. My own family business suffered somewhat because of my absence. I missed my kids' birthday parties a few times, PTA meetings, and other milestones. Am I proud of it? Absolutely not. Did my family understand and appreciate my attempts at making amends? YES!

Eventually, I decided that me taking all this time out to ensure other families were happy while together on a great vacation, was not worth losing time on momentous occasions with my own family. I eventually got to a point where I was no longer on a schedule, but was the one making schedules. I took that opportunity and seniority to ensure I spent most holidays with my family, much to their content. Today, my sons are older and in college. While I do feel guilty about all the important dates I missed with my family, the fact that my boys came through unscathed makes me feel a whole lot better about having worked so hard. Now, we get to spend holidays in fabulous places... and in swanky villas, too!

This industry isn't for everyone. The sacrifices made and the time-intensive dedication can sometimes hurt your family in unintended ways. Be prepared for that.

—I—
IT'S CALLED INFORMATION

The Christmas/New Year period is the busiest time of year on the island of Anguilla. Restaurants are hard to get into, beaches are a bit more crowded (although there are 33 of them to explore), traffic jams actually become "a thing", and celebrities flock to the jet-set haven with fury. For this same reason, many celeb stalkers also find their way to the shores of this tiny British island. And this brings me to my next bit of chuckles...

It was Boxing Day, and after a bit of a snafu on our very first week of opening a new villa resort, we had a last-minute availability. Lo and behold, on that very day, a couple with two toddlers walked into the lobby and asked if we took walk-ins. At first, I thought it was a bad joke. Who would fly to an island like Anguilla in the height of the "Festive" week with no prior hotel reservation? It was UNHEARD OF! But as luck would have it, we actually had an empty villa. We told the couple that we would rent half the villa to them for $3,000 a night... a very steep discount. They didn't blink twice, just whipped out their AMEX. We ran the payment for the first three nights, they checked in and then headed straight for the beach with babies in tow, strollers and all.

That evening, upon returning to the villa, they inquisitively asked the night staff multiple questions in rapid-fire succession: "So, where do you think Bill Clinton is staying?", "I heard Jay Z and Beyoncé are on that yacht out in the harbor...is it true?", "Is that Michael Jordan's jet parked at the airport? Where do you think he'll be going to dinner while he's on island?", "Does Al Gore usually stay on the West End?", "Could you call someone you know at another hotel and ask them if Denzel Washington really is having a dinner party tonight at that place down the street?" It was just question after question after question. I knew for a fact that they were first time visitors to the island, so I assumed they were just excited about the possibility of running into a celebrity. They always seemed poised to capture any celeb sighting with more cameras than a Nikon store!

The day finally came for this family of four to check-out. They left the island on a private jet at about 6 a.m., so their final guest charges were only run later that morning. BUT their credit card kept declining. I tried calling them and the numbers on their registration form seemed to be bogus, too. I started to panic and, in the chaos, I decided to Google their names. I was totally unprepared for what I discovered: they were a husband-and-wife celebrity paparazzi team! Their website was one of the hottest sources of online gossip at the time. It was unreal. They were literally famous gossipmongers.

All those "innocent" questions about celebrities had really been a ploy for information so they could get some "money shots." I was disgusted. Eventually, I did get their office manager on the phone, who gave me another credit card and their bill was paid in full.

But that day, I learned that Google could be quite an asset in this modern age of hospitality. Some may say it's spying, but as a professional, I beg to differ. For me, it actually helped me to know what I was dealing with. If I found out a guest was from a specific country, I would sometimes incorporate a welcome hors d'oeuvre with some of their native flavors, but with Caribbean flair. I've had instances where some guests were public personas with well-known preferences, such as a favorite flower or aperitif. Nothing felt better than seeing a huge smile on their face on arrival when a grand bouquet of gardenias brightened up their suites or the butler had a gimlet ready and waiting.

Personalized touches make guests feel special while making their overall experience unforgettable. Don't use the information as a stalkerazzi, but as a potential guide to making an extraordinary impression.

—J—
JUST SAY NO!

Well duh... of course this chapter is about drugs! It always amazes me how people seem to find drugs so quickly and easily when traveling in the Caribbean. The scariest part of all is that the people who look like they are walking the "straight and narrow" are usually the ones with the least inhibitions. Read on...

One of our guests had just flown to the island and settled into the most opulent villa with his family. He seemed to be a great guy and had been the lead contact during the pre-arrival planning. As an accountant, he spoke about his job often during telephone calls and just seemed like a typical dad and husband. For the first few days, he hardly left his wife and children's side. However, when he got on "island time", everything changed. He jogged down to the beach multiple times a day, alone. I often thought to myself, "What a health nut!".

One afternoon, a beach butler from a nearby resort walked into our Reception lobby and presented us with a Patek Philippe watch. He told us to give it to "the jogger." I asked him how he knew it belonged to that particular guest as we were at full occupancy. He smugly told me that the man had left his watch behind as a guarantee until he could get some cash. In my mind, I was like, "Cash for what?".

Being rather curious about that whole scenario, I asked what kind of arrangement was that. The beach guy grinned slyly and said, "De man wanted some heavier drugs than weed. So, we sent out to get more for him. But he take too long to come back wid de cash, so it done sell off to somebody else." With that, he handed me the expensive watch, bid me good afternoon, and left.

I stood there feeling dumbfounded. I eventually blinked myself back to reality and put the watch into an envelope to be delivered to the guest. What an eye-opener! I'd heard of guys who were gainfully employed at hotels all around the Caribbean, who literally earned twice their legal salary, from the sale of drugs, usually marijuana, and sometimes selling themselves too. (Ever heard of "Rent-a-Dread"?) To see a bit of this phenomenon up close and personal was a bit disconcerting. But such is the nature of the "hospitality beast."

In another experience, there was a multi-generational family staying at a villa celebrating a milestone. They wanted to end their trip with a bang, and we sure gave them one. We did a full poolside Caribbean BBQ event complete with unending rum punch, a live calypso band and tiki torches.

After a couple hours of dancing, eating, and gyrating, the crowd began to thin out as people went to bed. The principal guest, a New Yorker in his 40's, was the life of the party. When he noticed that it was down to only about six people left around the pool deck, he started yelling for people to wake up and come back down to the party.

He was loud and belligerent; we assumed he was just drunk. After being ignored for quite some time, he stomped off to his master suite and slammed the door. The staff took that as a cue to finish cleaning up the party zone... rapidly. Being the hands-on manager I've always been, I also joined the cleaning crew, picking up plates, wine glasses, cigar butts, etc.

As I moved towards a remote corner of the villa patio, a light went on inside the master suite bathroom and I saw Mr. Party Trooper in there. I realized at that point, he couldn't see out, but I could definitely see in. That wasn't the case in the daytime, when no one could see inside. Staff also rarely came to that side of the deck at night, so this experience was a definite first for me. I tried to scurry out of there before I saw anything that would be adversely etched in my memory forever.

With my hands full, I bumped into a chaise and dropped a wine glass. Cursing, as it broke into a gazillion pieces, I carefully stepped around the shards with my remaining items in hand, and went into the kitchen to get a broom and dustpan. When I went back to the same corner of the patio, the light was still on and I could see movement in the bathroom, but I tried my best not to look. When I finally felt like I'd swept up all possible pieces of glass, I turned to leave. As I walked away, in my peripheral vision, I saw a figure jumping up and down and heard pounding on the glass window. I swung around quickly and there was my bewildered-looking guest having a hissy fit by himself in the bathroom, kicking at air. But that wasn't the worst part. He was shirtless, with blots of white powder all over his nose and beard. He held a rolled-up item in one hand, like a straw, and on the bathroom sink was a thin mound of white dust. I couldn't stop staring! Sure enough, just like in the movies, this man had apparently been snorting cocaine! I was intrigued, scared, and sad in one giant ball of emotion.

I ran to the other side of the pool deck and saw the man's wife. I told her that I had been cleaning up on the other side and heard a lot of noise coming from the master suite. I suggested she check on her husband. I never told her what I saw. With a knowing sigh, she got up and went inside.

I heard yelling, cursing, and then sobbing. I never saw either guest again that night and the next morning, everything—and everyone—was back to normal. So many questions raced in my head: What if he'd overdosed? Where did he get cocaine from? Was this something he did at home regularly? Were his wife and kids in danger? But as with so many things we witness and observe while working in the industry, you just suck it up and keep doing your job until they leave. And then it's on to the next ride.

—K—

KATRINA, THE REALTOR FROM NEW YAWK

We all know that Katrina was a devastating category 5 hurricane that decimated Louisiana and other states in 2005. But what you couldn't possibly know is that I had to deal with a hurricane Katrina of a different kind. This Katrina was a realtor and an alleged socialite from New York who happened to be a repeat psychotic guest. She was so terrible that I am dedicating an entire chapter to her.

Katrina seemed to have it all. The status, the wealth, the looks, the picture-perfect family - a WASP mom on steroids (and opioids). Usually gracing us with her nauseating presence during the Christmas/New Year week in the Caribbean, she paid six figures per week for her private villa and often brought some A-list celebrity's kid with her as company for her teenaged sons.

My very first encounter with this woman left me baffled. As was customary, as the general manager, I would personally welcome the guests at some point during their stay. Katrina and her family had arrived on December 23 and it was only on Christmas morning that I realized I had not gone over to see them as yet. Because I knew they celebrated Christmas, I figured I'd go say hello right before noon, before they hopped in their golf cart and headed to the beach.

Around 11:30 a.m., I walked towards the villas with the Guest Services Manager who had built a rapport with Katrina and her husband. She told me they were just finishing opening their presents and it would be a great time to stop in and say hello. When we entered the building through the kitchen, I saw Katrina and her oldest son in the living room. He was sitting near the Christmas tree, opening a large white box with a scowl on his face and muttering to himself.

The Guest Services Manager gently spoke to Katrina, who sat with her back to us, and said, "Good morning, Katrina. Our GM is here to say hello."

Nothing happened. She repeated the greeting, a little louder this time, and waited for Katrina to acknowledge our presence. She did not.

At that point, I figured maybe she has ear pods in her ears or she literally couldn't hear us so I moved closer and said, "Good morning, Katrina. My name is Jeannine and I just wanted to welcome you and wish you a Merry Christmas. I hope you enjoy your stay with us." She continued to keep her back turned to us as if she had turned to stone.

At that moment, her son slammed the white gift box onto the floor and kicked it into the Christmas tree, breaking a few ornaments. While holding a plush light blue sweater in his hands, he yelled, "Why the fuck would you give me a sweater? We're in the fucking Caribbean! Are you dumb?"

He stomped off and went back downstairs to his suite. Katrina sat there unphased and said to the empty staircase, "Honey, why do you act like this? Come back here! It's going to be cold when we fly back to New York. Don't you like the color? It matches your eyes."

Mouths agape, the Guest Services Manager and I just stood there. Katrina finally stood up, smoothed her silk pants and her hair, breezed right past us and went into her master suite and closed the door. That was just a foreshadowing of things to come.

The next day, I was working in the office alone when I heard, "hello, hello," out in the main lobby. I quickly went out to see who it was. Katrina was standing there in all her Westchester County glory. Her fake Botox-induced smile brightly displayed, she asked me about booking her a day trip to St. Barths the next day where she would go on a luxury shopping spree. I told her I would find out if there was availability but needed to know if she wanted to sail or fly to the exclusive French island. She told me that she preferred to fly due to mo-tion sickness issues. I told her that she would have to pay a non-refundable 50% deposit to confirm the air charter because it was less than 24 hours away.

"You have our credit card number on file. Please use that to confirm the flight and send me all the details by email when it's confirmed," she said then turned around and sauntered out of the lobby.

I quickly noted the highlights of our conversation in the guest services logbook and proceeded to book her flight for a party of four. After sending her the email with all the details, I also sent a handwritten note confirming her 10 a.m. flight departure and 9:15 a.m. taxi pick-up details for the following day. The rest of the day proved fairly uneventful and I went home on time... a rare occurrence! But, alas, I think God was giving me a bit of a rest so I could deal with the drama of the next morning.

Upon arriving to work at 9 a.m. the following day, I read the logbook to see if anything exciting had happened the previous evening. Seeing no red flags, I glanced at my watch and made a mental note that the taxi would be here for Katrina and her family in about 10 minutes. I called the villa butler and asked her to relay the reminder to Katrina. She told me she would let Katrina know as soon as she saw her as no one had been up for breakfast as of yet that morning. Immediately concerned, I asked her if she was sure because that was highly unusual and their day trip to St. Barths was already set in stone. I asked the villa butler to knock on the master suite door to see if they were actually in there. She told me she'd call me back in a couple of minutes.

Now, this is where things turned crazy. My cell phone rang and I was told by the villa butler that no one was in the rooms. The morning housekeeper stated that the family had gone to breakfast at a neighboring beach resort and had rented cabanas for the day. My face flushed and I started to second guess myself, thinking, "Did this woman actually tell me to book this trip for today or was I mistaken?" I felt sick, thinking I could have made such a major error, but after I revisited my notes and replayed the previous day's conversation with Katrina in my head, I snapped out of my momentary stupor. I knew for a fact that this woman had to be the crazy one, not me.

Right at that moment, I got a call from the beach butler at the neighboring resort. When I answered the phone and listened to what he was saying, I felt my face immediately flush with shock. The beach butler told me that there was a deranged woman walking up and down the beach, swearing incessantly and saying, "That fucking idiot Jeannine! She booked us for a trip to St. Barths today when I TOLD HER to book it for tomorrow. What a stu-pid cunt! She will have to pay for our refund out of her own pocket!"

Paralyzed with anger, I recall hanging up the phone and pondered heading down to the beach to slap Katrina around. Then my plan was to immediately resign before I could be fired. First and foremost, I had not even spoken to this crazy bat that morning, but I was already very much aware of what she had done and was probably trying to cover her tracks with her husband who was allegedly "heavy handed" in many ways.

Just then, my boss appeared and proceeded to ask me what the hell had me shaking like a leaf. Taking a few deep breaths, I began to explain to him what had transpired. I happened to glance outside towards the courtyard and saw that the taxi was still waiting to pick up Katrina and her family. I walked out to the vehicle and paid the driver his fee from our petty cash and explained that the guests would not be going anywhere. I also called the airline from my cell phone to cancel the charter due to someone being unwell. (At that point, I didn't know what else to say.) Even though I knew the answer would be no, I even asked if there was any way they could get a refund. No dice.

I went back into the office and continued to explain to my boss what had transpired. I showed him the logbook notes and told him that it was only Katrina and me in the room at the time when she'd booked the trip the day before. I also pulled up the confirmation email that I'd sent to her and her email reply of just one word: "Awesome!"

He told me to handle it and walked away, looking amused. Maybe that wasn't the best advice. An hour later, I strolled into his office and admitted that I'd emailed the bitch and told her, in no uncertain terms, that she was to refrain from speaking negatively and maliciously about me to my colleagues to cover her own lies and manic insanity or I would sue her. I also included a copy of our emails from the day before and told her with glee that her non-refundable deposit of $2500 would be charged to her credit card by the airline that very hour.

(Now, believe me, I knew that this was not the professional thing to do and I can admit that. But in that moment, I honestly did not even care. We all have feelings and breaking points. No one calls me the C word and gets away with it. NO ONE!)

I firmly relayed to our CEO that I was prepared to be fired because I knew there would be backlash coming and I didn't want my actions to reflect badly on the property. He simply stared at me and told me to leave early to "go catch my breath." That was fine with me because the following day was also my day off. Two days of not having to deal with Madame Xanax sounded heavenly.

Two days later, I went to work and had a post-departure meeting with the staff about Katrina and her crass-as-hell family. I learned so many things at that meeting. For starters, the housekeeping staff said that they'd never seen someone with so many pills and how much of a challenge it was for them to clean her bathroom because of all the pills scattered along the counters. They made no attempt to put the pills back into any of the myriad prescription bottles. That was certainly an eye-opening revelation, but it made perfect sense considering the woman's behavior.

Another guest services staff member shared how Katrina was so afraid of her sons that she would ask the staff go into their rooms to wake them daily. Seeing the disrespectful manner in which her son treated her on Christmas morning, this was also not surprising.

The biggest shocker of all came when our CEO stuck his head into my office during our meeting and said, "Oh, I forgot to tell you, Katrina booked for the same time next year. She paid her deposit before she left. Her friends have a TV show in upstate New York and she promised to give us some free publicity when she goes on air next week. She never mentioned the St. Barths fiasco or your email to her, so I guess we can deal with that later." And then he was gone. Now THAT shocked the heck out of me.

My lesson from that ordeal was that when you're dealing with pill-popping, egotistical, psychologically unhinged, millionaires, sometimes keeping your cool may be impossible, but the outcomes aren't always as expected. Katrina and her family continued to visit regularly, but I always kept my distance.

—L—

LIVING LA VIDA LOLA

In an unassuming part of South Florida, there is a little oasis in the city, (ironically named) Hollywood: The Seminole Hard Rock Hotel and Casino—home of the world-renowned, architecturally iconic, Guitar Hotel. Long before making headlines as being the place where Ana Nicole Smith died, this property was legendary. Owned by the Seminole Tribe of Florida, the only unconquered Indian tribe in the United States, this hotel-casino is literally its own universe. As a sovereign nation, there are so many unique and awe-inspiring facts about the Seminoles, but this chapter isn't about that. (Do yourself a favor and research more about this tribe!).

In the summer of 2019, I was blessed to be an assistant manager on the launch management team for the Guitar Hotel's grand opening. If I said the hotel operations side during the pre-launch period was intense, that would be a gross understatement. Working 15-hour days, six days a week, was not uncommon. Ongoing construction, tight deadlines, influx of new staff, intense training, irate guests, and the usual chronic gamblers made for interesting times. Working at this hotel was different in many ways for me. While I'd worked in the upscale arena for most of my career, where guests and families were joyous and carefree 95% of the time, at this hotel, it was the reverse. Many of the guests were serious gamblers and when money is being lost by the nanosecond, people aren't exactly thrilled and happy. Leisure guests were few and far between at the time. Demands for upgrades and nonstop complaints of construction noise kept our phones buzzing around the clock. It was mentally and physically draining.

However, we did have some leisure guests who escaped to this enchanting destination very frequently for all the wrong reasons – and I don't mean gambling. Enter Mr. Juan Garcia Rodriguez. This dude was a serial cheater. He'd check into the hotel with his side-chicks and live it up like a rock star. At some point, one particular chick of the month, Lola Garcia, evolved into his woman of the season. They would stay at the hotel multiple times a month. Lucky for him, the hotel (like many others) had a special way of ensuring that guests who wanted their in-house status hidden could remain "unseen" in the reservation system. Mr. Garcia Rodriguez always opted to register his stays in this manner. Unfortunately for him, his wife also knew this trick.

One glorious day, when I was not at the property, a very irate Mrs. Garcia Rodriguez showed up at the Front Desk, with her 7-year-old son, demanding an extra key to her suite. When asked what her room number was, she said she didn't know it and stated that the front desk agent could just look up her husband's name in the system to get the room number that way.

The front desk agent asked her for her ID and her husband's name. Two things happened simultaneously at that moment: the agent found out this woman's name was ALSO Lola Garcia and her husband was technically unregistered in the system even though he was indeed a guest at the hotel. The hard part was trying to figure out if this man was actually at the hotel as the loving husband and father or shacked up with his side of beef aka the other Lola.

It didn't take too long for the real Mrs. Lola to start throwing a hissy fit and threatening the very new staff member. She told him that she knew her husband always registers to be "invisible", that he liked to get a non-smoking suite on a high floor, overlooking the pool, and always near the elevator. She insisted that she was staying with him in such a suite but after one too many mimosas at brunch, she couldn't find her key.

Attempts to contact Mr. Garcia Rodriguez discreetly to confirm this situation proved futile. In the end, based on the information in hand and on the computer screen, the agent made an extra room key and handed it to Lola. She trudged off, son in tow, and went to find her husband.

In less than five minutes, security scrambled to the 9th floor where chaos had erupted. The flabbergasted Juan encountered the tale of two Lola's that afternoon. Chuckling housekeepers recall getting a glimpse of the half-naked Mr. Juan being surprised and shocked when his wife opened the door to his suite while a very naked Miss Lola "Side Chick" Garcia screamed in assumed guilt or fear. Mrs. Lola threw her purse and heels at her husband while cursing the daylights out of her namesake nemesis... all while her son looked on in confusion.

The real VIP in the situation was Mr. Juan. He calmly told his girlfriend to get dressed and get her belongings while trying to appease his wife. When security arrived, they were beyond confused, but I think some of the men felt low-key admiration for papi chulo Juan. I mean a man like that must be a genius to have a wife and a girlfriend with the same name, right?

In the end, Juan led his girlfriend out of the suite, as staff and other guests looked on, and told his screaming wife that she could enjoy the room for the rest of the day with their son. He left her standing there fuming and strolled down the hall with his Louis Vuitton duffel bag swinging. Pretty crappy guy, but this saga definitely made for another unforgettable moment in hotel operations history.

—M—

MAUNDAYS BAY
MIRACLE

In early January 2015, my husband was very sick. We had been to several doctors and with his symptoms of chronic fatigue, dizziness, numbness in the extremities and insanely high blood pressure, yet no one could pinpoint what was going on. His blood labs were fine and outside of having a damaged optical nerve show up on his MRI, no one could figure out what was happening. One doctor told us that if we eventually found out what was wrong, we should update him because he was curious to know himself. Another female doctor started googling his symptoms when we visited her office. It was heartbreaking. Can you imagine having a doctor telling you to let him know your diagnosis because he was clueless? We were beyond stressed out at that point.

The third doctor we saw told us that we needed to find a neurologist ASAP. Being on a small island, specialists were very hard to see immediately unless you flew to another island or the U.S. mainland. In this case, to make matters worse, all of the doctors had advised my husband not to fly. The earliest appointment we could get to see a neurologist on the island would be in approximately two months.

It was a tough time for our family. Due to my husband's health challenges and him being unable to run our own family business, I decided to work remotely for two weeks. I set up a makeshift office in our bedroom and worked by his side daily.

On January 15th, I had to sign the payroll checks and decided it would be good to head into the office at the hotel for a bit and go through the pile I knew was gathering on my desk. My mother-in-law, who was alive and well at the time (we would sadly lose her in 2016 to cervical cancer), told me she'd come spend the entire day with her son so that I could go off to work. She said as long as I was back by 6:30 p.m. it would be fine because she was going to prayer meeting at her church at 7 p.m. I told her I would be home long before then.

But despite my earnest intentions I wound up being late getting home that day—and with good reason.

I got lost in the mountain of tasks that had been on desk and catching up with the team on several fronts. I ordered in lunch and asked not to be disturbed in the afternoon so I could leave around 5. By the time I looked up from my computer, it was getting dark outside. I glanced at my watch and it was almost 6:30 p.m.! I frantically gathered my laptop and the remaining folders and documents that I needed to review.

As I rushed out of my office door, hands full, trying to find my car keys simultaneously, I literally bumped into my boss who was just returning to the property for a dinner meeting with a client. Papers scattered. I barely managed to catch my laptop before it hit the ground. Flustered and in tears, I felt like my life was like those papers on the floor. My emotions were scattered in so many directions.

Not being one to crack under pressure, my boss was duly concerned and asked me how my husband was doing and what was the latest update on his health. I told him that the MRI was completed and the frantic doctor visits over the past couple of weeks had proven futile as no one knew what was wrong. I further explained to him that we needed to see a neurologist but the earliest appointment I could get would be in six weeks. He gasped and told me that everything would work out and that I could take all the time I needed to deal with this. I tried to choke back the hot tears that spilled from my eyes as I bid him good night and started to leave the office.

At that moment, I saw a bright light outside and a rental car pulled up alongside our signature garden attraction, a marble fishpond with cascading waterfalls under a hardwood trellis. The 10-foot structure was designed to look like huge fish jumping out of a pond. The ornamental marble fish made for quite the selfie background and many of our guests took photos there to remember their vacation. As late as I was and as emotionally drained as I was in that moment, I wiped my face, put all my mental junk aside and went outside with a dazzling smile into the night.

I saw three women taking photos of each other in front of the landmark. Transforming into hospitality Wonder Woman mode, I offered to take a photo of all three of them together. They happily obliged, and after taking a few photos of them, we chatted for a bit. They were bubbly and kind, not appearing to be in a rush. I asked them where they were going for dinner and how was their stay so far. It was at that moment that the radiant blonde asked me if I was Jeannine. I said yes, and she said, "I remember you... but haven't seen you this trip. This is my sister and our friend. It's their first time here and we leave tomorrow morning. I'm glad we got to see you. How have you been?"

I turned to the two beautiful, smiling brunettes and said I hoped they'd had a great vacation. I tried to be brief and very lighthearted as I told her I'd been working from home because my husband wasn't feeling great and we'd been to a lot of doctor appointments in recent weeks. Trying to take the spotlight off of myself, I teasingly told them that since they'd had such a great time, they should extend their stay for a few more days.

The first woman turned to me and said, "Oh, I wish! But we can't. My sister has to get back to work. She's a doctor."

I turned to the cheerful doctor and said, "I've seen so many doctors recently. I can imagine how busy you must be. What kind of doctor are you?"

The next three words to come out of her mouth left me in a blubbering, snot fest mess.

She said, "I'm a neurologist."

I literally buckled in that moment and started crying profusely. Of course, these three women had no idea why I was crying so one of them asked, "What's wrong? You don't like neurologists?"

I tried to compose myself and in a fit of verbal vomit, I shared that my husband needed to see a neurologist immediately but there were none readily available on island, my husband couldn't fly to see one anywhere else, and the next one was only arriving to the island in six weeks. They stood there silently as I wept openly.

That's when my newfound angel spoke and said, "We leave at 9 a.m. tomorrow. Please bring your husband to see me at 8 o'clock tomorrow morning. I'm not doing this in any official capacity, but I'd love to meet him."

I had to refrain from hugging her on the spot. I told her we'd be there in the morning and wished them a fabulous evening. I ran back into the office and crying freely now, rushed to find my boss. He heard me bawling before he saw me. When I pushed open his office door, he was standing behind his desk. He asked me what was wrong, but I could barely get the words out.

I stammered, "The women, one of the women... she is a doctor... she's the doctor I need. OH MY GOD IN HEAVEN! She's the doctor..."

He sat down in his chair with a thud and said, "Don't you dare tell me what you're trying to say is that you just found a neurologist. Jeannine, was she a neurologist?!" I nodded frantically and ran out to my car with my briefcase and laptop. I didn't even say goodbye; I sped out of the parking lot. All I could think about was getting home to tell my husband the GREAT news.

The next morning, we got to the property at 7 a.m. My usual modus operandi is, "be one hour early versus being even one minute late." In this situation, that mantra was especially important to me. I walked down to the villa and waved to one of the breakfast service staff. I told her to let the guests know that I was on property. In the blink of an eye, my angel-doctor came to the foyer and said, "Is your husband here? I'll see him in your office." I told her that I would be ready for her to meet him as soon as she finished her breakfast. She told me, "No. Breakfast can wait." I was speechless. What manner of SUPER woman was this?

We both walked to my office building together. Her sister soon followed. I was a wreck. I had no idea about what a neurologist could possibly find or diagnose, but my own online research was pretty scary. Once we got to the office building, I introduced her to my husband, and they hit it off immediately. She asked if she could use one of the empty breakout rooms to do the "examination."

I opened it up and left them to it. I was pacing the floors and the doctor's sister saw how anxious I was. She walked up to me and said, "Listen, do you trust me? I want you to trust me. Trust me when I tell you this. My sister is the BEST at what she does. She will be able to give you some answers. Don't worry, just trust that it will be okay." I just nodded and smiled through my nervous-happy tears. I couldn't believe this was happening. It was surreal.

At that moment, the doctor came out to where I was standing and asked if I could get her a flashlight. Our hurricane supply closet was in another building, and I didn't have the keys. I ran from office to office and cupboard to cupboard in the admin building looking for a flashlight. When I couldn't find one, I tried to call my boss who was not in office that morning but didn't get him. His office was usually locked but I figured I'd try the door anyway. When I pushed on the handle, it easily gave way. Surprised, I opened the door and, as if put there by angels from above, a blue flashlight was sitting in the center of his desk. The only reason I know no one else could have overheard the conversation and put it there, was because there was no one else in that building! I grabbed it, in sheer disbelief, and went to give it to Doc.

Ten minutes later she and my husband emerged looking hopeful. She discussed what she thought his condition could be and what we could do to alleviate some of his symptoms immediately. She asked if she could speak to my primary care doctor, who just happened to own his own private mini-hospital on the island. I called him right away, quickly explained what had taken place and gave her the phone. In medical-speak they had a brief conversation and then she handed me back the phone.

My doctor told me that I would have to purchase five vials of a specific medication that was only sold at the main government hospital. He would have the prescription ready for me to pick up and I would take it to the hospital. After I got the vials, I was to return to his office so we could chart the way forward.

My husband and I were so humbled, overwhelmed, and overjoyed in that moment. We bear-hugged angel-doc and her angel-sister and thanked them repeatedly for caring so much and being our much-needed miracle. They left the property at 9 a.m. on the dot that day, but they left as my forever friends and not just guests. To this day, we are still friends and try to get together whenever possible. (And may I add that the miracle didn't end there? When we got to the hospital to purchase the vials, they only had five vials in stock and would not be able to get more for three weeks. I carried those vials like precious babies in my hands until we returned to my PCP and turned them over to him. My husband proceeded to have a 5-day intravenous treatment akin to getting chemo. Our amazing and thoughtful doctor opened his clinic to us even on the weekend so that my husband would have his Thursday to Monday treatment in the fastest possible time.)

To this day, I cannot wrap my head around everything that happened that January. All I know is that I am forever grateful and I will always believe in miracles.

ACKNOWLEDGMENTS

Thank you to my Heavenly Father from whom all blessings flow.

I take this brief opportunity to thank my wonderful family for always encouraging me to write, write, write.

To my patient, kind, adoring husband who has tolerated my manic writing moods for over 20 years, I say GRACIAS.

To my AMAZING sons who were often tucked away in my office doing homework at any given property, I love you and this is for you!

To my mom, Annette; siblings, Jenelle, Joselle and Jamie; and to my cousin, Charanell, thank you all for believing in me and my writing skills since I was a bratty kid.

To my travel family, Lisa and Ron, where should we go next?

Special shout out to my elementary school librarian, Ms. Oliver, who let me check out 10 books at a time, even while scolding me for doing so.

To the Smith family and the Sheriva crew, you're forever my family. Sheridan, Toya and Ton—I hope some of these stories make you smile.

To Natalie, Felicia, and Suzanne—the powerhouse trio—and family, I owe you so much; I'm blessed to call you my extended family.

Dr. Lowell Hughes, of Hughes Medical Center, you're a rare gem. Thank you for all you do. Proud to call you my cousin and godbrother!

To my ever supportive, caring, loving, encouraging friends and family all around the world, I love you like I love sitting on a beach in Anguilla with a good book. (I dare not list names for fear of forgetting anyone near and dear to my huge heart.) **THANK YOU!**

JEANNINE CONNOR GITTENS was born and raised on St. Croix, US Virgin Islands to Anguillian parents. She is a small business owner, Realtor, Spanish teacher, 80's music fanatic, hodophile and self-certified "beach bum." Having enjoyed a successful career in hospitality spanning many zip codes and area codes, her adopted motto of, "Love All, Serve All," rings true in all she does. She spends her time between her homes in the Caribbean and Florida, and prefers to "*catch flights, not feelings.*"